Washington
from the air

WHITE STAR
PUBLISHERS

Washington
from the air

CONTENTS

© 2003 White Star S.r.l.
Via C. Sassone, 22/24
13100 Vercelli, Italy
www.whitestar.it

TRANSLATION
Studio Traduzioni Vecchia - Milan, Italy

ISBN 88-540-0016-7
Reprints:
1 2 3 4 5 6   07 06 05 04 03

Printed in Korea
Color separation by Fotomec - Turin

Text
Elysa Fazzino

Photographs
Antonio Attini

Graphic Design
Maria Cucchi

1 In 1783 Congress decided to dedicate an equestrian statute to George Washington The obelisk, completed over 100 years later in 1884, is considered to be a more impressive monument.

2 Mars on a horse with Valor, a female figure, at his side. This is one of the two gilded bronze equestrian sculptures, "The Arts of War," at the entrance of the Arlington Memorial Bridge.

3-6 Ferryboats ply the Potomac in the evening, passing the lighted monuments.

7 The neo-classical Thomas Jefferson Memorial, situated on the Potomac Tidal Basin, honors the author of the Declaration of Independence, later the third President of the United States.

8-9 The Mall begins below the Capitol. Foreground left is the Supreme Court; to the right, the Senate office buildings, connected to the Capitol by a subway train.

INTRODUCTION

10 top A park with trees isolates the White House from downtown buildings. The street between the president's residence and the oval meadow is closed to traffic as a security measure.

10-11 Washington's even roof-line is broken only by the obelisk dedicated to George Washington. Capitol Hill can be glimpsed in the background.

11 top Alexandria, a former tobacco port, maintains its 18th-century look with gracious houses and charming inns lining the bank of the Potomac.

11 bottom The Georgian-style Mount Vernon, 15 miles (24 km) from the capital, was George Washington's much-loved home and retreat; here he experimented with new crops on his family's plantation.

Washington, D.C. is a monument transformed into a city, the history of America distilled into a memorial; it is sacred ground bearing the most significant symbols and vestiges of a history as brief as it is magnificent. The city is the incarnation in marble of the values expressed in the Declaration of Independence and in the United States Constitution, the ideals of democracy and freedom, and the right to bear arms to defend them. The Capital is the patriotic apotheosis of the virtues that transformed an offshoot of colonial Europe into the greatest power in the world. The great urban stage projects a theatrical design of symbols that Americans proudly display. But behind the marble- and stone-clad façades that reflect the images and reflections of classical civilization move the mechanisms of the most sophisticated political machine in the world. Washington: *caput mun-* *di*, capital of the federal government, soil of the American supremacy, has its political mind in the White House and in Congress while its military arm is the Pentagon. Cosmopolitan for the functions it performs, the city is host to embassies and international institutions, it remains American to the core for the thousands of citizens who work for the public good, either directly or indirectly. Politics, with its business and its contracts, is the activity that drives an economic zone, home to the 5.4 million people who live between the District of Columbia and the suburbs. In peace as in war, it is the city that flies the largest number of flags and jealously retains the old Stars and Stripes that inspired the national anthem. Once every four years, Washington becomes the capital of high society. Those who count in America are invited to the new president's inaugural balls, a whirlwind of dances with ladies in long dresses and gentlemen in tuxedos

12 *The satellite view shows how the Potomac separates the District of Columbia (occupying the area top left), characterized by straight lines, from Virginia (bottom right-hand corner), with the Pentagon just visible beyond the river.*

13 *Washington is located at the junction of the Potomac (to the right) and the Anacostia (below). The layout of the city's monument-marked center is clearly visible.*

14-15 *The founders dreamed of a thriving port, protected by the embrace of the two rivers and surrounded by lush hillsides, as the photograph suggests. However, over time, the original river-city identity has gradually faded.*

16-17 *An elevator and an 897-step stairway both lead to the Washington Monument's pyramidal summit, where eight windows provide panoramic views over the city.*

18-19 *A commercial port in the 18th century, Georgetown is the capital's oldest neighborhood. After the mills and foundries had left, it was saved from decay and declared a national historic site.*

20-21 *The Pentagon was built in record time between 1941 and 1943 for the Department of Defense. The construction involved more than 1,000 architects and 14,000 workers.*

12

in the salons of the luxurious hotels, museums, and federal buildings. Stars of stage and screen entertain VIPs and others. From the edges of the empire the pro-consuls who raised funds and votes arrive to pay homage to the new Caesar. The city is indisputably a center of espionage; from Washington the tentacles of the CIA, the FBI, and other federal intelligence agencies spread out across the nation and the world. That's why the agents of foreign espionage services constantly pound the avenues and streets of the city and its sub-

urbs. The aura that surrounds this theater of action generates substantial business for a highly popular spy museum and for ex-agents who lead spy tours through the streets, areas and houses through which they passed – presumably without leaving any traces – as the 007s of the most famous intrigues. The capital encompasses far more than the Mall and its great stone and marble buildings: it includes downtown's classy restaurants, Georgetown's trendy cafés and boutiques, the jazz clubs on U Street — where Duke Ellington

once lived — as well as the military marches of John Philip Sousa and the National Symphony Orchestra's concerts at Kennedy Center. Buses casually take tourists from the sacred to the profane, from Arlington National Cemetery to shopping in Pentagon City. Kayaks skim along the Potomac as bicycles wheel along the paths beside it, fathers and mothers exercise by rapidly pushing baby carriages that resemble Harley-Davidsons, and the joggers in shorts run wherever there are shady sidewalks. All this – and much more –

is Washington "No country has ever before had the opportunity to deliberately decide where to have its capital city ..." wrote Pierre L'Enfant to President Washington in 1789. Washington is a capital created on paper by a political choice, not promoted to that role over the slow evolution of centuries and civilizations. The French architect planned to leave space "for the enlargement and embellishment that the increase in the wealth of the nation would allow it to create" in a future that was then still far off. That future has now arrived.

HISTORY

Halls of power that recall the white temples of Greek and Roman antiquity, broad tree-lined boulevards that delineate the green fields, the tranquil Potomac that runs at a tempo slower than time: This is Washington, as different as one can imagine from the clichés of large American cities. No dizzying frenzy, no skyscrapers, a skyline that does not try to reach the sky but rather emphasizes the horizon with snow-white symbols of the greatest modern experiment in democracy. Well-proportioned, reassuring buildings, icons of harmony and equilibrium, structures that give citizens space to open their spirits and minds to the values of the Fathers of the Country.

Here, between Capitol Hill and the White House, beats the political heart of the nation.

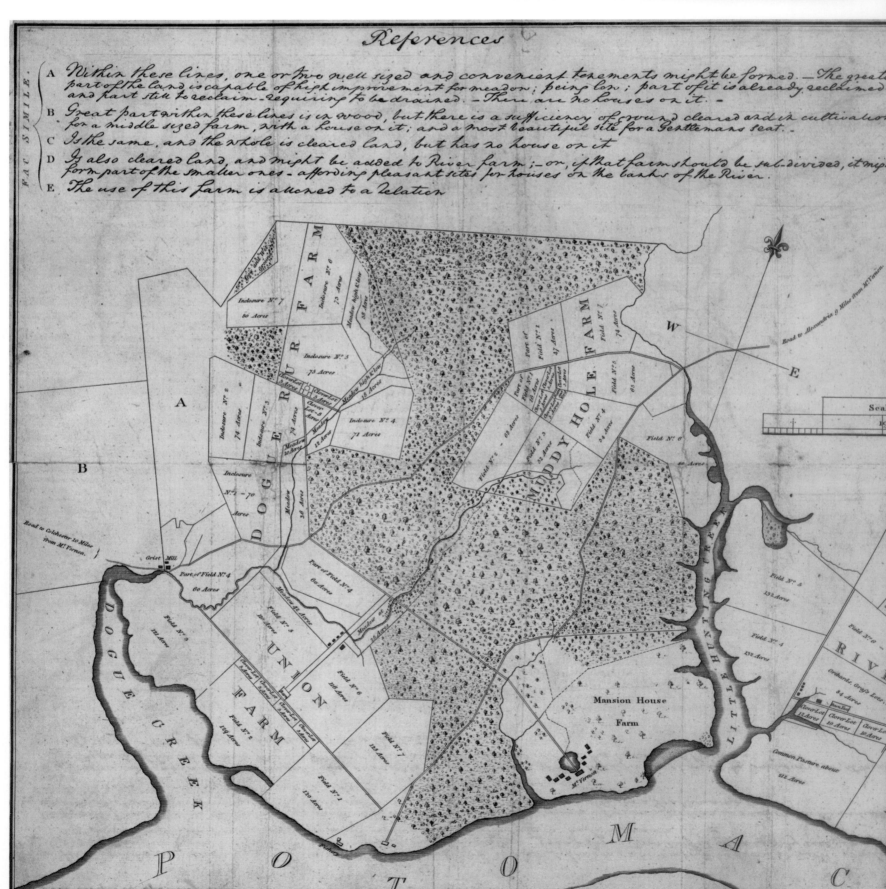

From the farthest corners of the United States, starred-and-striped Americans come as if on a pilgrimage, eager to confirm the rites of patriotism before the many memorials. Proud yet subdued, they stand before the statue of Lincoln, the white marble obelisk dedicated to Washington, and the black marble wall commemorating the servicemen killed in the Vietnam War.

Created for politics, the city of Washington began with a uniquely political compromise at the bargaining table. After the War of Independence, the Congress – which had begun meeting in Philadelphia – decided that it was necessary to find a place to build the new federal capital. The Founding Fathers did not want an overly powerful city, fearing that the government would end up being influenced by anything but disinterested pressures. The

would agree to locate the capital in the South, on the banks of the Potomac. In 1790, Congress conferred on President George Washington the task of choosing the site, and Washington chose a place at the confluence of the Potomac and Anacostia rivers, an almost entirely rural area that until many years later was called "Wilderness City." This location, immersed in the southern culture and economy, had the advantage

24-25 George Washington's estate at Mount Vernon included land that could not be cultivated, covered by swamps and woodland. This map, made in 1801, is based on a drawing by the general.

25

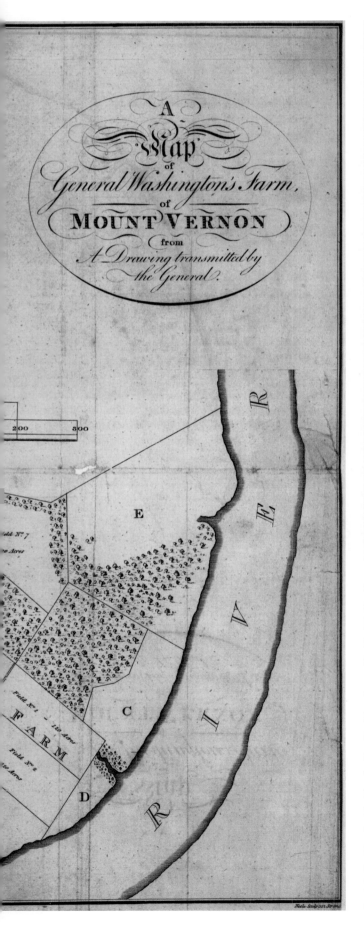

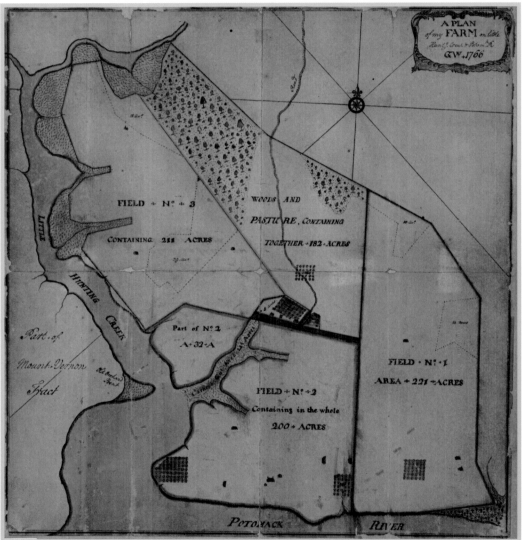

states of the North and the South disputed the issue in the first hints of the conflict of interest that would explode decades later into the Civil War.

An agreement between Thomas Jefferson and Alexander Hamilton to exchange votes in Congress was settled upon at a dinner, where choice dishes and a velvety Madeira played an instrumental role. This solution was that the southern states would vote to assume the war debts of the ex-colonies at the federal level, accepting taxation to pay the larger debts of the North. In exchange, the northern states

of being geographically in the middle of the coastal states. It was also in a strategic position for commercial exchanges, being close to the rivers, a bay and the ocean. And *dulcis in fundo*, the site was only a few miles from President Washington's plantations in Virginia, from his beloved Mount Vernon home. From this fine house, even now, posterity can admire intact the panorama of the valley that descends to the Potomac, a view very dear to the first president and maintained over the centuries by a ban on building anything there.

25 George Washington himself drew a handwritten plan in 1766 of the farm land that he had purchased between Little Hunting Creek on the Potomac, near his Mount Vernon estate

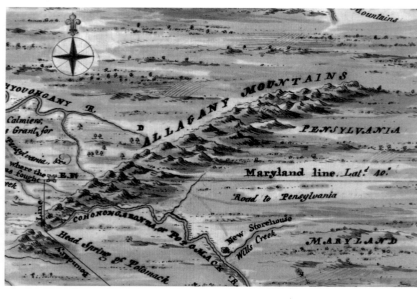

Maryland and Virginia ceded the land, respectively giving up the villages of Georgetown and Alexandria, important ports for the tobacco trade. The original parcel of the Federal District – later called the District of Columbia in honor of Christopher Columbus - was a square, ten miles on each side, with angles pointed toward the four cardinal points, north, south, east and west. There were one hundred square miles of real estate, for the most part farms held by nineteen families. To build the federal capital, each single parcel had to be purchased, with negotiations that involved speculation and perhaps even bribes. Even today it is still remembered that, right to the end, David Burnes did not want to sell. He owned a large piece of land that ended at the base of Capitol Hill. Even worse, he had just built his cottage, and he resisted to the bitter end. The kindest story says that Burnes was convinced to cooperate after a personal conversation with Washington. But other documents suggest that he was offered a considerable amount of money to induce him to follow more reasonable recommendations.

To measure and mark the boundaries, Washington hired Andrew Ellicott. Assigned to help him was Benjamin Banneker, an Afro-American from Philadelphia, esteemed as a mathematician and astronomer. Between 1791 and 1792, with simple instruments, the two made a topographical survey of surprising accuracy and placed forty large milestones along the edges of the future capital. However, to transform this land into the much dreamed-of city was not at all simple. Controversies and political squabbles impeded the original project and, for many years, the city remained unfinished.

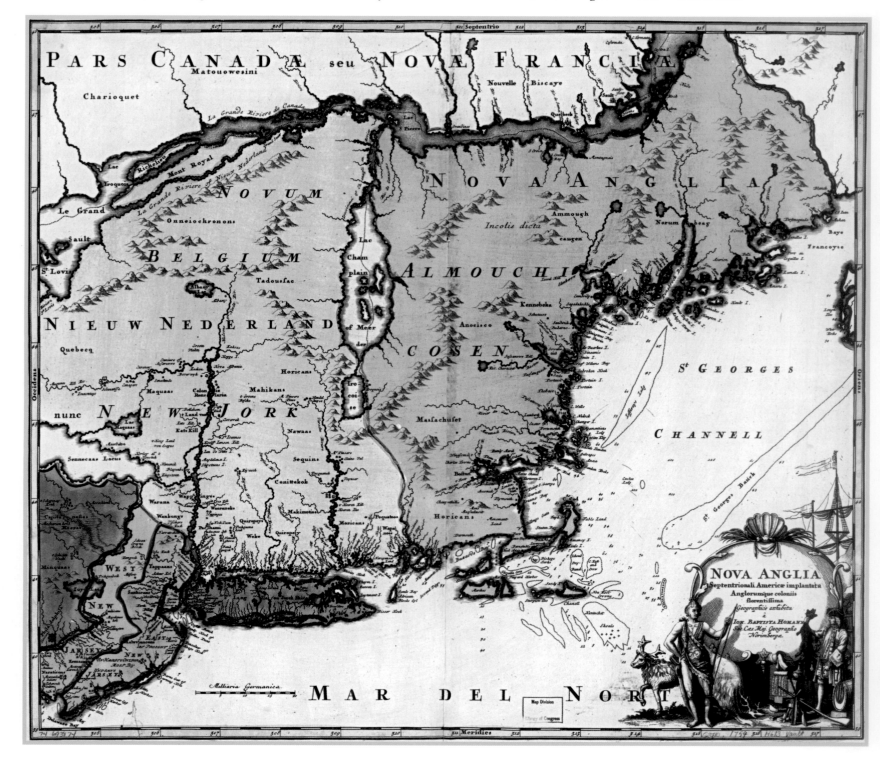

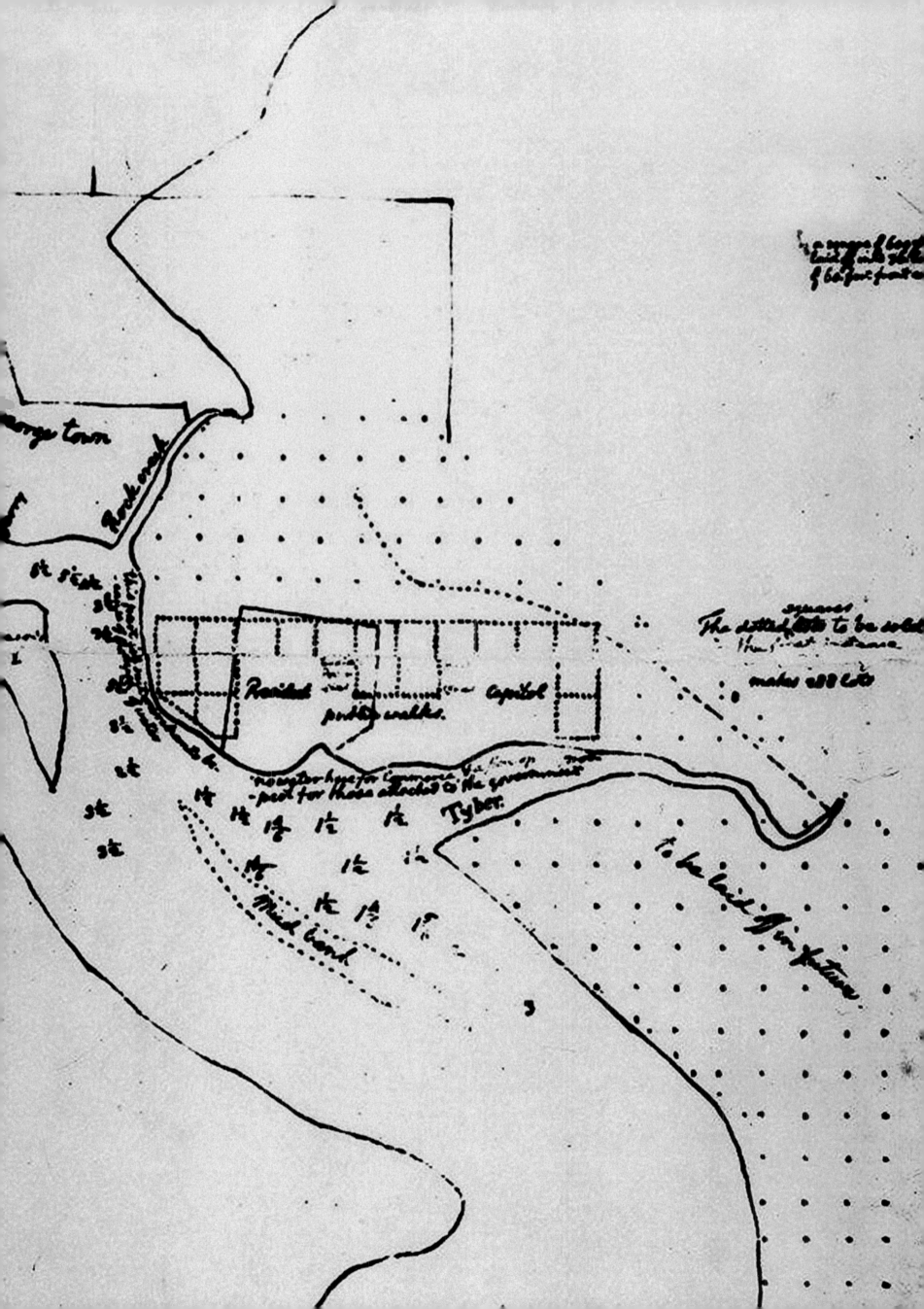

In the rigorous geometry of the monumental center, softened by gardens in the style of Versailles, we glimpse Pierre L'Enfant's "great vision." L'Enfant was a French architect and engineer who fought in the American Revolution under George Washington. In 1791 L'Enfant, son of a painter to the French king and, like Lafayette, an inflamed supporter of the American cause, was given the job of planning the capital of the new nation. On the battlefields, he had absorbed its ideals and ambitions – freedom, first of all, but also the opening of new frontiers, the yearning for space, the sense of community.

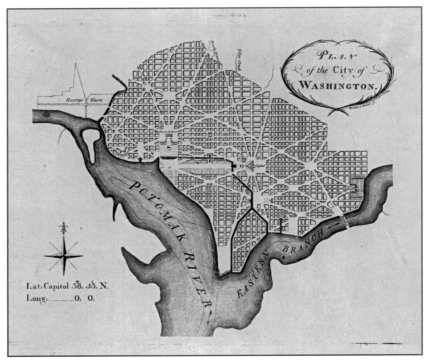

However, his first impression of the place was not idyllic. He later recounted that he arrived in the midst of "heavy rain, thick fog, mud and marshes," contributing to spreading the belief that Washington was built on swamps. The humidity and suffocating heat of the place led the European diplomatic corps to list the American capital among the hardship assignments until the age of air-conditioning arrived. But these were not the concerns of its founders. Inspired by his Paris, the city planner designed the axes and avenues for a huge city, a masterpiece that was to symbolize the entire country.

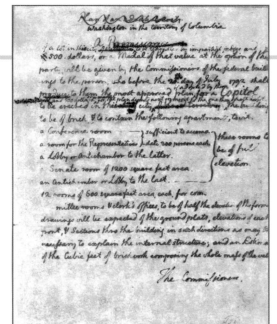

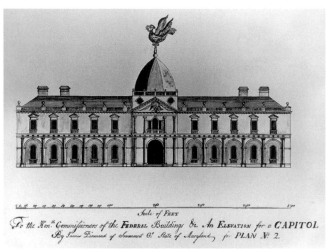

29

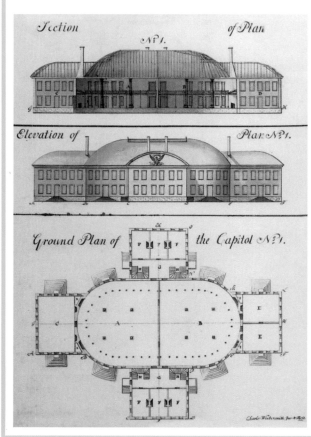

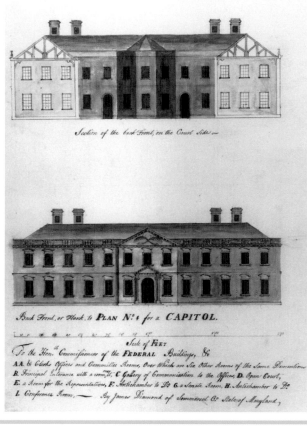

L'Enfant's plan revolved around a triangle made up of the Congress (the Capitol), the presidential palace (the White House) and an equestrian statue of George Washington on the banks of the Potomac. A large boulevard 425 feet wide — an immense width for that period — encircled by gardens was to lead from Capitol Hill to the Washington Monument. This is now the Mall. A ceremonial boulevard, a diagonal, was to connect the Capitol and the White House, the legislative power and the executive power, which would be able to see each other from the two ends of the boulevard. Four boulevards radiated from Capitol Hill — one

being the Mall — dividing the city into four quadrants. The streets running north and south were designated by numerals, beginning with one, while those running east and west were given the letters of the alphabet.

An ambitious design, it envisioned a megalopolis. What was labeled the "City of Magnificent Distances" foreshadowed a future then unimaginable for the village of that time, which had a little over three thousand souls. L'Enfant never saw the completion of his work. He quickly antagonized his clients. He was accused of being stubborn and arrogant, of not staying within the limits of his budget and of not

wanting to subject himself to the authority of the three administrators who were supervising the project. He was fired in 1792. It is said that, when he left, he took his plans with him. But the imprint of this misunderstood champion of American "grandeur" remained. The versions contradict each other, and history is mixed with legend. What is, however, certain is that six months after L'Enfant's departure, Thomas Jefferson hired Ellicott, the topographer, to carry out the plans for the city, based on the designs of the French architect. Some say that it was Banneker who recreated L'Enfant's plans, reproducing them entirely from memory.

28-29 George Washington, his wife Martha and their grandchildren Nellie and Washington Curtis, portrayed in his Mount Vernon home.

28 bottom This city plan of Washington was made by the French architect Pierre Charles L'Enfant in 1792.

29 top left Jefferson himself wrote the draft of this announcement publicizing the national competition for designing the Congress building.

29 bottom left In the 1792 competition for Capitol Hill, the German engineer Charles Wintersmith presented this design.

29 top right The eagle on Capitol Hill was proposed by James Diamond in 1792.

29 bottom right James Diamond's 1792 design for the Capitol was based on a Renaissance palazzo model.

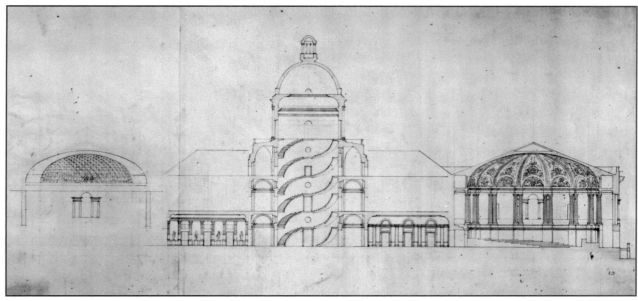

30 top Benjamin Henry Latrobe modified William Thornton's prize-winning design.

30 center The plan of the viewing level in the Capitol Rotunda shows the interior stairway and the decorated dome.

30-31 President Washington liked Thornton's project for its "grandeur, simplicity and convenience.

31 top Influenced by Parisian avenues, Jefferson wanted rows of poplars along Pennsylvania Avenue.

In any case, both Washington and Jefferson endorsed these plans as the official map of the city without giving any recognition to their creator. And like many unfortunate artists, L'Enfant died in poverty, without glory. Posthumous recognition arrived decades later. His designs were rediscovered toward the end of the 1800s with the advent of the industrial age, a time when Washington wanted to give itself an appearance consonant with its role as the capital of a nation that, by then, was a world power. L'Enfant's remains were

then exhumed from a pauper's graveyard and interred in Arlington National Cemetery. He enjoys the ultimate tribute: from his tomb, the visitor can see all of Washington, the fruit of his "vision."

Despite misfortunes, Congress was able to establish itself in the city in 1800, the year in which the capital was transferred from Philadelphia to Washington. The building on Capitol Hill was still under construction, but that didn't matter much. In November of that year, the representatives met for the first time in their new home. Washington was not, however, the splendid city designed by L'Enfant. It was called it the "capital of the miserable huts" and the "mud pit." Cattle chewed their cud on the streets of dirt, dust or mud, depending on the weather. There was no running water or sewers, and garbage could be seen at every turn. The war against Great Britain only made things worse.

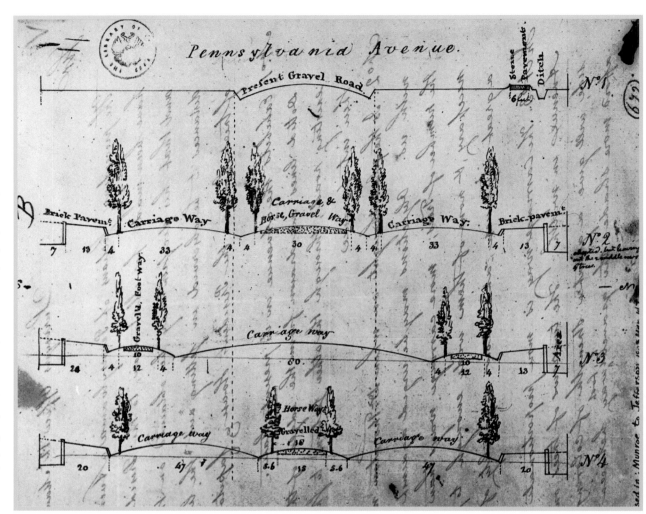

32 and 33
Washington, D.C.
was captured and
burned on 24
August 1814 during
the war between the
United States and
Great Britain.

The print to the left
shows the British
forces attacking
from the Potomac
under the command
of General Ross
(right).

On August 24, 1814, British troops under the command of General Ross and Admiral Cockburn invaded the weakly defended city and set fire to the Capitol, the White House and almost all of the public buildings. A providential storm impeded what would have been the total destruction of the structures. The damage, however, was so great that there was for reconstruction over abandonment. After visiting Washington in 1844, the great English writer Charles Dickens defined it as the "City of Magnificent Intentions," marked by spacious boulevards that begin from nothing and lead to nowhere."

The initial enthusiasm was by then only a memory. Discontent spread to Alexandria and Georgetown. The people complained about economic loss and champed at the bit for a return to the jurisdiction of the states that had ceded land to create the federal district. In 1846, the inhabitants of Alexandria could crow victory. Congress decided to restore to Virginia all the land

south of the Potomac that the state had donated. On the other hand, it is said that Georgetown's hope to be returned failed only because Maryland did not want its land back.

In those prosaic years, however, an Englishman, James Smithson, believed in the future of Washington. Although he never set foot in America, he gave his name to what became an unrivaled treasure of the capital, the Smithsonian Institute. The illegitimate son of Hugh Smithson, Duke of Northumberland, and Elizabeth Hungerford Keate Macie, a widow of royal blood, Smithson was born in France in 1765 and spent his entire life in Europe. A scientist and philosopher, an enthusiast of chemistry and mineralogy, he was (but only at the age of fifty) finally authorized by the British Crown to bear his father's name but not his title. From his mother's family, he had inherited a considerable fortune and, in his will, he left it to the American people to found an institute "for the development and

diffusion of knowledge among men" in Washington. After a long fight with the family, the United States won and in 1846 Congress established the Smithsonian Institute. Smithson's motives remain a mystery. Perhaps he considered America as the illegitimate progeny of Mother England and therefore with a destiny similar to his own. Certainly, however, he showed more faith in Washington than did many of its inhabitants.

The Civil War created the conditions for growth that transformed the derided "Wilderness City" into a true capital. Divided between the southern spirit of its inhabitants and the northern calling of its government, Washington had abolished the sale of slaves in 1850, but not their possession. Two years before, the city had experienced the first massive attempt at flight in the history of black emancipation – the Pearl Affair. On the evening of April 15, 1848, seventy-seven slaves silently slipped away from their homes, rooming houses and hotels and embarked on the

schooner *Pearl*, which was waiting on the Potomac to carry them to freedom in New Jersey. But severe weather blocked the schooner, which was quickly discovered by the posse in pursuit of the fugitives. The slaves surrendered and were then exposed in chains to the anger of the whites.

The outbreak of the Civil War saw families divided, with brothers enlisted on opposite sides. But Washington had to give an example and, in 1862, Congress abolished slavery in the District in symbolic anticipation of the rest of the nation. Defended by a chain of fortresses along its southern perimeter and on the Union's front lines, the capital was transformed into a military camp. Within were the General Staff and the troops, the hospital for the wounded on Capitol Hill, and the arms factories: it was a beehive of military activity. South of the Potomac, ever more bloody battles were fought against the Confederates. After the war, the population had nearly doubled, with the presence of 40,000 freed slaves.

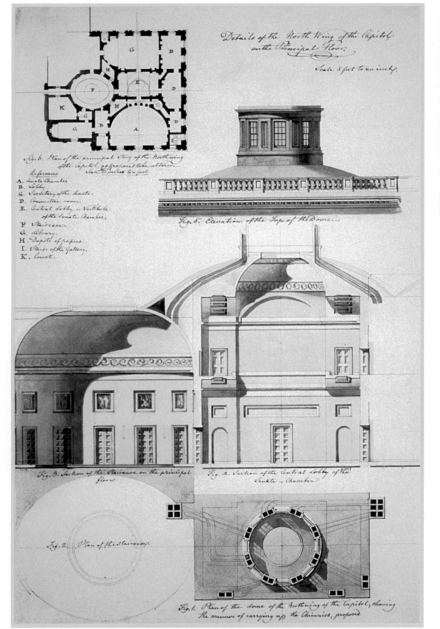

34 top In the 1874
project by the famous
architect of gardens
Frederick Law
Olmsted, the area
around the Capitol is
beautified by small
streets, paths, trees,
fountains and
terraces.

34 bottom
This drawing, done
by Benjamin Henry
Latrobe in 1814,
shows the layout
and projected view
of the design for
the north wing
of the Capitol.

34-35 Washington
in about 1856. The
panoramic bird's-eye
view from the west,
with the new dome
of the Capitol in the
forefront, is the
work of Edward
Sachse.

36-37 This view of
Washington from the
Potomac, looking
north, dates back to
about 1880 The
obelisk of the
Washington
Monument can be
seen in the forefront.

COPYRIGHT 188

Farragut Sq. (NORTH WEST DIV.)　Scott Place. Louise Home　Mc Pherson Space　Columbian University. Howard University

Arlington House　Department of Justice.　14th St. Circle　Liberty Sq.　K St. Market　Massachusetts Av.　City Hall Park

Lafayette Sq.　Foundry M.E. Ch.　Ebbitt House　U.S. Patent Office　U.S. Post Office　Metropolitan Hotel

Corcoran Art Gallery　EXECUTIVE MANSION　U.S. TREASURY　Riggs House　Pension Bureau　Census Bureau　Washington Market

WAR, NAVY & STATE BLDG.　(WHITE HOUSE.)

NATIONAL OBSERVATORY　Rawlins' Square　(SOUTH WEST DIV.)　The President's Grounds　Willard's Hotel.　Washington Monument　The Mall　Agricultural Dpt. Smithso

Bureau of Engraving & Printing

POTOMAC RIVER

THE CITY OF

BIRDS-EYE VIEW FROM TH

DRAWN BY C.R.PARSONS.

	Stanton Sq.	(NORTH EAST DIV.)		
ent Printing Office			Lincoln Sq.	Kendall Green
l Hotel Pennsylvania Av.	B.&O.R.R.Depot	THE CAPITOL	Seward Sq.	U.S. Marine Barracks
tute National Musuem B.&P.R.R.Depot	Botanical Garden			Navy Yard
LONG BRIDGE	Jefferson School	(SOUTH EAST DIV.)	U.S. Arsenal	EAST BRANCH OF THE POTOMAC

WASHINGTON.

POTOMAC - LOOKING NORTH.

38

38 bottom This 1883 plate map shows Washington from the river and includes Georgetown, Foggy Bottom, and the waterfront along the Potomac.

38-39 This map of Washington made in 1921 dubbed the city the "Beautiful Capital of the Nation." Union Station's railroad tracks are visible alongside Capitol Hill.

New houses and buildings, roads and parks arose. From 1870, Alexander Shepard, nicknamed the Boss, guided the urban development that made people forget Washington's rural reputation. The capital began to be defined as "the show place" of the nation, the window in which its wealth, power and progress could be seen. The "grandeur" that L'Enfant yearned for finally had what was needed for it to become a reality. Architects and engineers found inspiration and guidance in L'Enfant's plans, and

they built the large government buildings, the monuments and the museums, blending the original impulse with the exigencies of modernity. "Make no little plans.

They don't have the magic to make men's blood boil," advised the Chicago architect, Daniel Burnham in 1900, when the McMillan Commission was preparing to revive L'Enfant's plans. And indeed there is his Union Station, a neo-classical jewel of the Belle Epoque, considered by many to be the most elegant railway station in America.

There is also the Library of Congress, the gigantic jewelry box that aspires to collect everything written, an intellectual powerhouse and beacon for all the libraries in the world.

The drive for the beautiful and grand accelerated in the 1920s and 1930s, was fed by the public works program during the Great Depression, and continued during World War II and in the postwar boom. That war began a new growth phase for the population of Washington. The capital became crowded and it expanded. Its first airport was built, the National Gallery of Art was opened, and the city enriched itself over the years with everything that was still lacking. These included the Capital Beltway ring road; the Kennedy Center, an ambitious complex for concerts and performances; and the National Cathedral, a traditional Gothic-style place of worship under construction for ninety years.

Across the Potomac River in Virginia, the Pentagon was completed in 1943. it remains the largest office-fortress in the world, and today only one smoke-blackened stone set in the reconstructed façade recalls the terror strike of September 11, 2001, the watershed that divided the recent memory of Washingtonians and all Americans between "before" and "after."

40-41 top This
aerial view shows
the Washington
Monument (left)
rising from the Mall.
The Mall was
reconsidered in the
McMillan
Commission's 1901
plan, which returned
to Pierre L'Enfant's
original idea.

40-41 center This
1905 bird's-eye view
presents most of the
city of Washington.
Visible to the left is
the oval field and in
the background to
the right is Capitol
Hill.

40-41 bottom A
panoramic view of
Capitol Hill in 1912
from the top of the
Washington
Monument. Below
and slightly to the
left is the National
Museum of Natural
History.

The history of the capital is, in large part, the story of the nation. Facts and places are those of the American epic. The White House has seen a succession of presidents whose names and achievements every American schoolchild must learn.

Congress and the Supreme Court enact large and small political battles in the eternal tension among the three powers—executive, legislative and judicial. The city's sites become extraordinary because they are touched and forever changed by extraordinary events. Think of the red brick of Ford's Theater, where President Abraham Lincoln was shot to death, the rounded mass of Watergate, where the scandal erupted that drove Richard Nixon to resign, the long perspective of the Mall, re-echoing the words of Martin Luther King "I have a dream ...," the protests of Vietnam War marchers, the demands of the blacks in the Million Man March.

Having been for over two centuries at the head of a nation that gathers so many others under the protective wing of the eagle that symbolizes it, Washington perfectly interprets and reflects a certain psychological habit of the American people. Created out of nothing, thwarted and even derided, the city has not yielded to the attacks of history, succeeding with tenacity, industriousness, inventiveness and courage to win the respect and glory that a new, great world capital deserves.

42-43 This 1939 aerial photographs shows the Jefferson Building of the Library of Congress in the forefront and the east front of the Capitol in the background. The Senate wing is to the right, the House wing to the left

43 The Yankee Clipper photographed during its inaugural flight over Washington on 3 March 1939 when it was "christened" by the First Lady. With 74 passengers it was the "jumbo jet" of the period.

44 The march on Washington on 28 August 1963 brought over 250,000 demonstrators together in front of the Lincoln Memorial. They demanded civil rights legislation and immediate abolition of segregation in schools.

44-45 In taking the inaugural oath in front of the Capitol at the inception of his 1953 and 1957 presidential terms, Dwight Eisenhower used the Bible his mother had given him when he graduated from West Point.

46 left Black men from all over America gathered on the Mall on 16 October 1985 for the Million Man March. It was led by Louis Farrakhan, an Islamic leader, to promote the African-American cause.

46 right On 11 October 1986 thousands of people publicly displayed the AIDS Quilt to commemorate AIDS victims. Seen here is the quilt, made of 38,000 sections bearing the names of more than 70,000 people killed by the disease, extending over the Mall to the Capitol.

47 An aerial photograph of 12 March 2002 shows the Pentagon's damaged western section. On 11 September 2001, terrorists flew the hijacked American Airlines Flight 77 into the building; the tragedy of took 189 lives.

THE MALL

Washington: an ideal Renaissance city transposed into the New World, created with the neophyte determination of a nascent democracy and with the pride of a power that wants to be exemplary. Architectural symmetry, rationality of space, grids with grand perspectives: a unity that instills harmony and balance, a *res publica* that revolves around a human intelligence, and a layout that guides and inspires.

"A hill rises in the high country ...," wrote Tomaso Campanella in imagining the City of the Sun. And there it is, Capitol Hill, the new Campidoglio, the knoll immediately perceived by the French architect Pierre L'Enfant as "a pedestal awaiting a superstructure," the high ground destined to host the sanctuary of the republic, the site of the Congress of the United States. A symbolic representation of the utopian union of good government, knowledge and nature, "the federal enclave" embraces the

past, the present and even the future of the United States. Here democracy works through victories and defeats in dialectical confrontations among the Capitol, the Supreme Court, and the White House. Two hundred years of history unfold in the esplanade of the Mall with its memorials erected as a perennial reminder of the great men and women who made America and of the soldiers, sailors, and airforce personnel – today both men and women — who died for her. Art and science exhibit their

artifacts in museums that are the last link, the most visible one, to the research carried out and ongoing in all fields of knowledge,

This procession through the noblest allegories of the American myth begins from the heights of Capitol Hill where the legislative and judicial powers of the country are concentrated. The fulcrum of the capital's radial design, point of origin for the long perspective of the Mall, the Hill dominates the city with the most spectacular monument of the

50 top Located in the Capitol until the British burned it down in 1814, the Library of Congress now it has three buildings. Seen here are the Jefferson Building and, below, the Adams Building.

50 bottom Congressional staff had to rent offices in nearby buildings until majestic office bocks were built on both sides of the Hill at the beginning of the 20th century.

51 For over two centuries, the Congress (the House of Representatives and the Senate) has held sessions in the Capitol. The Mall and the major avenues of the national capital radiate out from Capitol Hill.

capital, the massive white structure of the federal parliament.

The majestic Rotonda, crowned by its cupola, in turn surmounted by a statue of Liberty, the two wings of the House of Representatives and the Senate: the unmistakable mark of the real industry of the capital – politics. Sculptures in high relief celebrate "the genius of America": Democracy and Progress. Paintings exalt the salient moments in American history: the landing of Christopher Columbus and the Declaration of Independence. The capital even has its "Michelangelo," a Roman painter, Costantino Brumidi, who frescoed the inside of the cupola with a transfigured "apotheosis of Washington." He died tragically following a disastrous fall from the scaffolding while he was painting a frieze in the Rotonda. A political exile from Papal Rome, he is credited with these words which express all the hope felt for the new nation. "My only dream," he said, "is to decorate the capitol of the only nation in the world where there is freedom." The Supreme Court building has stood since 1935 in sight of the Capitol. After decades of occupying temporary locations, the Court established itself in its solemn white marble building, constructed on the model of a Greek temple. The juxtaposition of the two institutions seems to translate into physical space the maxim

on the pediment: "Equal justice under law." Nine judges, nominated by the president and confirmed by the Senate, judge the constitutionality of laws and have the final say in disputes that concern rights guaranteed by the Constitution. When it wishes to exert its power, the Court is far-reaching and has had a profound impact on society with its watershed decisions on issues such as racial segregation, the death penalty, and abortion. It should not, therefore, be surprising that the confirmation of nominees to the Supreme Court are often the subject of memorable power struggles. The nine judges, nominated for life, can dictate the law, even in politics.

In Washington's evocative geometry, Capitol Hill is at the acute angle of a right triangle. The hypotenuse of Pennsylvania Avenue leads directly to the other angle, the White House.

52 and 53 The Washington Monument is 230 feet (69 m) high and weighs 90,854 tons. Its walls are covered in marble and range from 15 feet (4.5 m) in thickness at the base to 18 inches (45 cm) at the peak.

54-55 The words of the Gettysburg Address, delivered in 1863, are incised on the walls of the Lincoln Memorial. In reiterating that "all men are created equal," the president prepared the nation for the abolition of slavery.

56-57 The open green areas around the Washington Monument have been used for military parades, peace marches, liberal demonstrations, festivals and ceremonies of all types.

58 There is no better view of the Capitol than from the Washington Monument. From its peak, there is also a stunning view of the Reflecting Pool and the Lincoln Memorial.

59 From the White House's North Portico, the exiting president and the president-elect leave together and share part of the walk to the inauguration ceremony on Capitol Hill.

60-61 The semicircular Southern Portico of the White House was added in 1824. In 1948, President Truman had a balcony built for his private apartments, inciting fierce criticism.

62-63 The White House lights stay on at night in the heart of the capital. Though a symbol of the American presidency and the nation's power, the house is architecturally and stylistically simple.

From here, the perpendicular line (with the Ellipse) descends, leading to the third angle, marked by the obelisk dedicated to George Washington. The horizontal line, which closes the figure, is the broad swathe of the Mall. This is the "grand avenue" conceived by L'Enfant in 1791. He envisioned a large public space for the amusement of the people, a tree-lined promenade next to gardens and public buildings, embassies, theaters and academies. For the first fifty years, the Mall remained little more than a muddy street. Toward the end of the 1800s, buffalo even roamed there in the first attempt to create a national zoo.

But after the McMillan Plan in 1901, the Mall began to be transformed into something much closer to what L'Enfant had envisioned. It is a place of remembrances but, unlike a mausoleum, it pulses with life. Children and adolescents go there to play in the fields, kicking around balls or flying kites. Workers from nearby offices willingly sit down for a break on the grass. The tourists going in and out of the museums are a constant presence,

and Washingtonians themselves often spend Sundays there.

A red "castle" with nine towers heralds the largest cultural complex on the planet – the Smithsonian Institute, which over the years has multiplied its inheritance from the English scientist James Smithson in order to offer public museums that make the head spin. The most popular one is the National Space and Air Museum, with the Wright Brothers' *Kitty Hawk* of 1903; the famous *Spirit of St. Louis*, in which Charles Lindbergh made the first flight across the Atlantic; and the Apollo 11 space capsule. And then there is the National Gallery of Art, with Henry Moore's bronze inundated by light at the entrance to the East Building, Calder's mobiles and Miró's tapestry. The largest blue diamond in the world, the fabulous Hope Diamond, has made the fortune of the Museum of Natural History since 1958. Many Americans, however, blame the gem – which is supposed to be cursed – for all the negative events that have happened to the United States since it became a national treasure.

The monument on the Mall to the first president. George Washington, is a hollow-core white marble obelisk, 558 feet high, the only "skyscraper" in the capital. It

is the only structure in the area whose height admittedly exceeds that of the Capitol. No one is allowed to build higher than the capitol, not even by erecting an antenna. Abraham Lincoln is enthroned in the memorial in front of the Reflecting Pool, the site of many demonstrations and marches, which has witnessed, even in the darkest years, the freedom of speech guaranteed by the First Amendment to the Constitution. Thomas Jefferson is commemorated by an immense bronze statue in a circular temple with Ionic columns and a cupola of white marble, inspired by his dwelling in Monticello The Jefferson Memorial stands on the shore of the Tidal Basin, the body of water that in the spring reflects the pink of the cherry blossoms. Thousands of those fallen in the Vietnam War have their names inscribed on the low walls of polished black granite that run along the sides of a tranquil and shaded path.

The White House rises on agricultural land that David Burnes originally did not want to sell. When George Washington finally convinced him to give up the parcel designated for the home of the president, the unyielding landown-

er continued planting in the middle of the road next to his nearby farm. The cornerstone of the White House was laid in 1792, and until the Civil War, it was the largest home in America.

Except for George Washington, all the presidents of the United States have lived there. The original building was destroyed in 1814, in the fire set by the British army. Only a portrait of Washington was saved from the original furnishings, snatched from the flames by Dolly Madison, the beautiful and inventive First Lady of those years. She was the only woman to do the honors of the house under two presidents, Thomas Jefferson, who was a widower and trusted to her good taste, and James Madison, her husband.

According to legend, the walls of the dwelling were then painted white to mask the signs of the fire. The prayer of John Adams, who moved into the White House in November 1800, when it was not yet finished, is inscribed on the marble fireplace in the official dining room: "I pray that Heaven bestow blessings on this house and on all those who live here in the future. May only honest, wise men govern under this roof."

64 The steps of the Jefferson Memorial often seat enthusiastic crowds who listen and applaud bands that play patriotic music.

65 In 1912 Japan made a gift of the first 3,000 cherry trees planted around the Tidal Basin. Later 171 trees had to be removed to clear ground for the Jefferson Memorial, but another thousand trees were planted when the work was finished.

66-67 Inspired by the Pantheon in Rome, the Jefferson Memorial is an American interpretation of Neoclassical style. The president/architect would have liked it; he introduced the circular colonnade to the United States.

68-69 Behind the columns of his Memorial, Jefferson's statue looks toward the White House. This was at his request to emphasize that he would make sure the presidents remained faithful to the principles of the Constitution.

70-71 *The Arts and Industries Building of the Smithsonian was built in 1881 to exhibit objects from the Centennial Exposition. Near the "Castle," it houses temporary shows.*

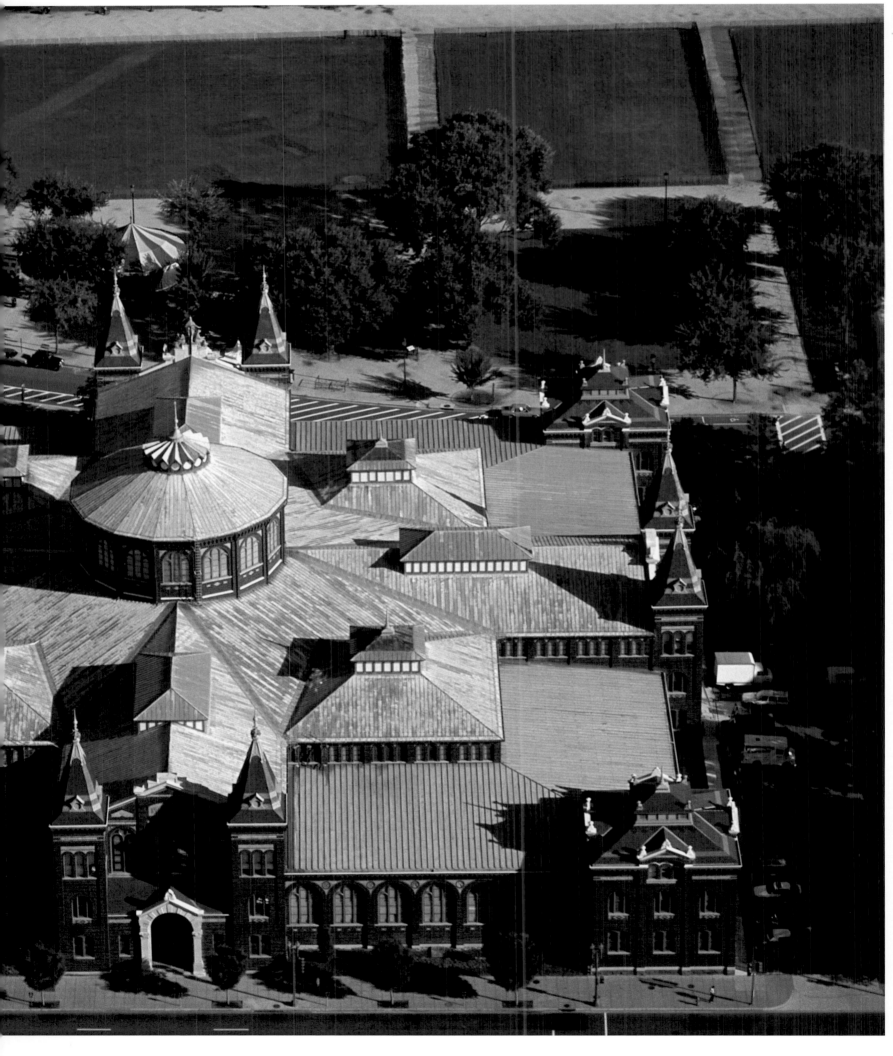

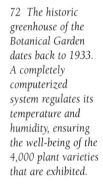

72 The historic greenhouse of the Botanical Garden dates back to 1933. A completely computerized system regulates its temperature and humidity, ensuring the well-being of the 4,000 plant varieties that are exhibited.

72-73 Dinosaurs and fossils are not the National Museum of Natural History's only treasures; it also features a very popular gem collection that includes the Hope Diamond and more than 1000 other gems.

73 bottom The Neoclassical style of the West Building of the National Gallery of Art stands out in the row of institutional buildings on the Mall.

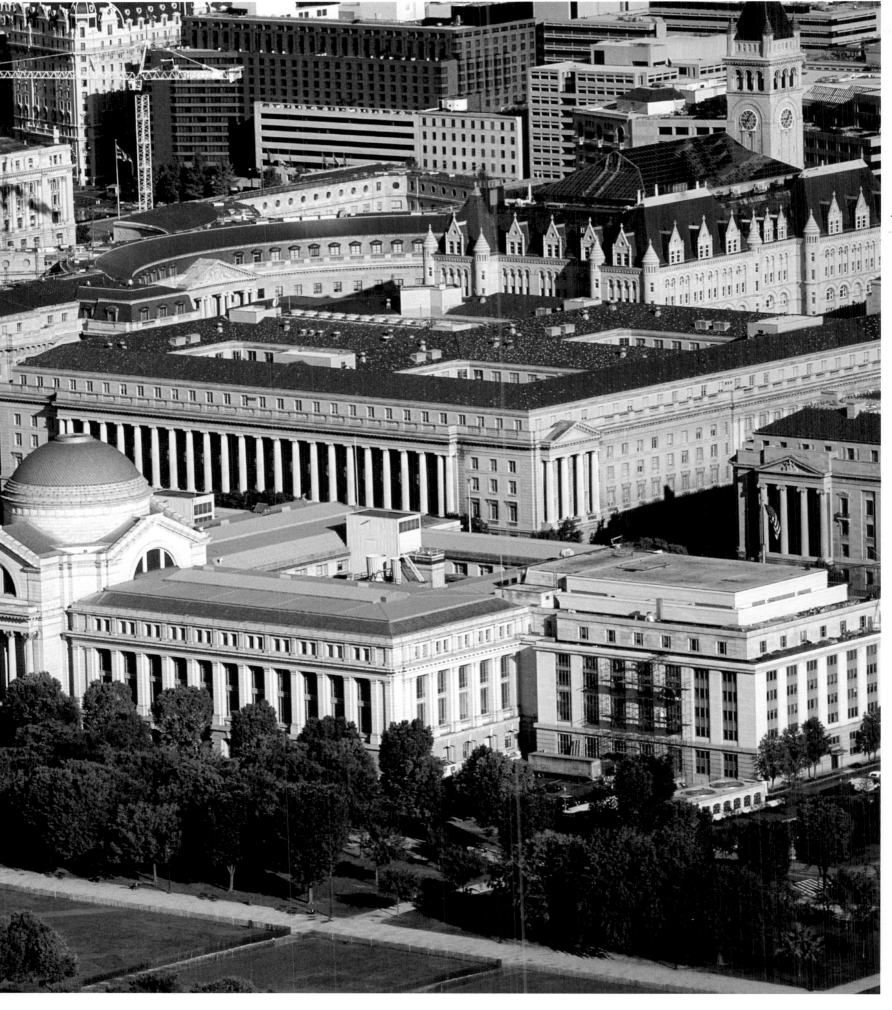

74 *The first visitors crossed the threshold of the Franklin Delano Roosevelt Memorial immediately after its inauguration on 2 May 1997.*

75 The Roosevelt
Memorial fits in well
with West Potomac
Park, honoring the
president who led the
United States out of
the Depression and
successfully through
World War II.

76 War and Peace
side by side: on the
avenue near the
Arlington Memorial
Bridge are copies of
the equestrian
sculptures, "The
Arts of Peace."
"Music and
Harvest," and
"Aspiration and
Literature" (in the
top photograph) are
featured.

77 The two
Neoclassical
sculptures "The Arts
of War," called
"Valor" and
"Sacrifice," were
financed by Italy in
a celebration of the
friendship between
the two nations.

78-79 The entrance
to the Arlington
Memorial Bridge,
with its monumental
equestrian statues,
marks the entry to
the capital and to
the monuments and
symbols of the Mall.

80-81 The
Arlington Memorial
Bridge is considered
the symbolic bridge
between the North
and the South:
unites the
monument of
Lincoln, a
northerner, with the
Arlington House, in
Virginia, dedicated
to the Southern
general, Robert Lee.

THE CITY

In typical American big-city style Downtown is a forest of cement-and-glass blocks for administration and business, anonymous parallelepipeds housing offices and apartments, as well as large hotels from an earlier age and elegant buildings saved from degradation. Washington, too, has its modern center, the metropolitan navel where people work and do business, its core crowded with elegant shops and luxurious restau-rants. Adjacent to the monumental heart of the city, Downtown extends around the White House and pulses between Connecticut Avenue and K Street. It borders on restored historical quarters, now vibrating with life, such as Dupont Circle, which teems with antique shops and bookstores, and Adams Morgan whose exotic locales and ethnic cuisines attract crowds at night.

Neo-classical hints are also found here in buildings that con-

84-85 Old and new developments follow one after the other in the capital's modern neighborhoods; they form a vibrant urban center of offices, hotels, restaurants and shops.

84 bottom The Library of Congress is located next to the Supreme Court; it contains more than 120 million items, including books, records, photos, maps and manuscripts.

85 top The tower of the Old Post Office Pavilion overlooks national museums and government departments. A statue in the lobby commemorates Benjamin Franklin, who started the U.S. Postal Service.

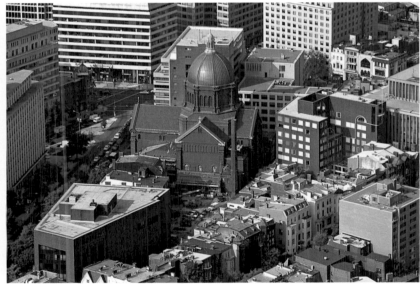

join the political symbols of the capital and the structures devoted to daily affairs. An example is Union Station, which paradoxically brings to mind the magnificent past of Greece and Rome, even though at the beginning of the 20th-century railroads signified modernity and progress. Its architect, Daniel Burnham, in looking for a "noble and dignified" style for the train station close to the Capital, took the Baths of Diocletian in Rome as a model, using porticos and arches, Ionic columns, and sculpted figures representing Fire, Electricity, Agriculture, and Mechanics. Within the structure, after decades of decay, the luxury and elegance of the Belle Epoque has been returned to its original splendor, with the Main Hall and its barrel-vaulted ceiling allowing natural light to enter, illuminating its gilding and marble and statues of Roman legionnaires.

With few exceptions – and one of these is the white marble building of the Corcoran Gallery – Downtown is more interesting because of what happens there than for its architecture. This is the case with the headquarters of the Federal Bureau of Investigation, the FBI, a cement tenement that attracts the curious because it issues the list of the "Ten Most Wanted" criminals. The square offices of the International Monetary Fund and the World Bank are well

85 bottom The mass for John Kennedy's funeral was held in St. Matthew's Cathedral in 1963. Every year, the "Red Mass" is celebrated with the participation of the highest governmental officials.

known by now. A malicious theory suggests that the area between the White House and the river is called Foggy Bottom perhaps because of the murky politics, but it is more likely named after a swamp that once existed there. A name, a destiny: it is here that the rounded complex of the Watergate Building stands, the gray memento of the scandal that led President Richard Nixon to re-sign. It was in this complex of hotel rooms, residences and offices that, in 1972, the Democratic Party's electoral committee suffered the break-in that led to the investigation made by the *Washington Post* reporters, Bob Woodward and Carl Bernstein.

Close to Watergate is the Kennedy Center, recognized for its fine concerts and performances. The Center is dedicated to the Democratic president who defeated Nixon and who was later assassinated and mourned. The simple, austere marble building faces the Potomac, and encloses interiors of fanciful modernity. It is in harmony with the style and elegance of Kennedy's First Lady, Jacqueline Bouvier, who wanted to make Washington a cultural as well as a political capital.

86-87 To the immediate left on Pennsylvania Avenue are the buildings of the National Gallery of Modern Art, one contemporary and one neoclassical.

87 The Catholic church of St. Peter's is a short walk from Capitol Hill and draws many senators and representatives. It is renowned for its acoustics, which are perfect for religious music.

88-89 Between the Neoclassical colonnades of the Bureau of Engraving and Printing and the red bricks of the Victorian-style Auditor's Building, the hexagonal Hall of Remembrance of the Holocaust Museum commemorates the Nazis' victims.

90-91 Fourteenth Street is one of the largest thoroughfares running through an area of administration buildings. To the left, the Annex Building of the Bureau of Engraving and Printing.

92-93 The FBI's headquarters (front left) on the north side of Pennsylvania Avenue. It is named after long-time FBI director J. Edgar Hoover, who died in 1972.

94 The Ronald
Reagan Building
and International
Trade Center
accommodate
conferences, events,
fairs, and even the
political satire of the
Capitol Steps
troupe.

95 In its glory
days, Union Station
was a mini-city with
saunas, a swimming
pool, bowling lanes,
a hotel, a police
station, butcher,
baker, medical
officer and even a
mortuary.

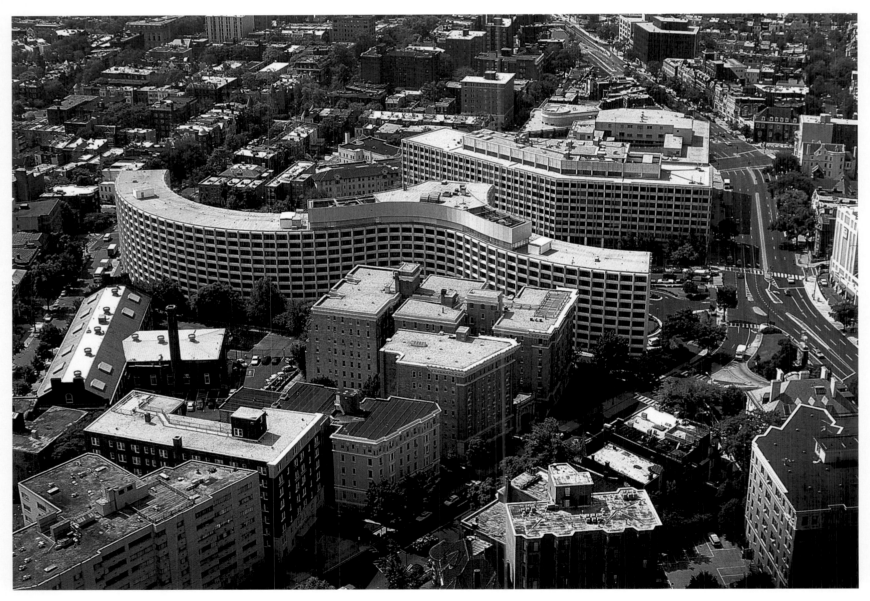

96 Contemporary shapes and classical references alternate seamlessly in the area of public buildings and museums around Capitol Hill.

97 top At the intersection between 17th and M Street, the site of the National Geographic Society can be seen in the forefront with its two buildings, the Explorers' Hall and the Grosvenor Auditorium.

97 bottom In front of the curved building of the Hilton Hotel, John Hinkley shot President Ronald Reagan in 1981. The bullet stopped one inch from his heart.

98-99 Connecticut Avenue cuts through the city center to the residential suburbs. To accommodate in-bound and out-bound rush-hour traffic, lanes change direction at given times.

100 Howard University, a mainstay of African-American higher education, was founded by General Oliver Otis Howard of Civil War fame, who wanted it to be "beyond all segregation."

101 Not all the 19th-century row houses around Capitol Hill have been torn down. Some still survive in middle-class and student neighborhoods.

102-103 It is common to see people enjoying the fresh air under the wooden porches in front of their houses, a custom in the southern states that survives in working-class neighborhoods.

104 top and
104-105 Orderly
lines of small colorful
row houses punctuate
the urban space of an
old residential
neighborhood in the
capital.

105 top
Washington's
distinctive Islamic
Center of
Washington sits
within a verdant
oasis.

105 bottom Trinity
College was founded
in 1897 as a
Catholic university
for women. Notre
Dame Chapel, right,
hosted Pope John
Paul II in 1979.

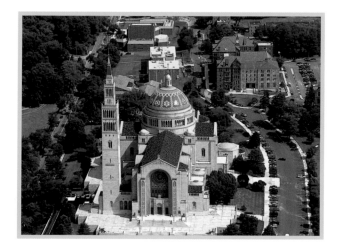

106 top The Basilica of the National Shrine of the Immaculate Conception honors the Virgin Mary, proclaimed "the patron saint of the United States" by Pope Pius IX in 1847.

106 bottom The Byzantine tradition of early Christianity survives in architecture and mosaics in the Basilica of the National Shrine. The crypt evokes the catacombs.

107 Every year, thousands of Catholics from around the world make a pilgrimage to the National Shrine. The tiara used in Pope Paul VI's enthronement is kept here.

108 top The National Cathedral, in richly decorated Gothic style, is one of the world's largest cathedral. The idea of a "large national church" was already part of the city plan in 1792.

108 bottom The funerals of Presidents Woodrow Wilson and Dwight Eisenhower were held in the National Cathedral. Martin Luther King made his last speech from its pulpit.

108-109 It took 90 years to build the National Cathedral. Italian artists and artisans made important contributions to decorating its interior and façades.

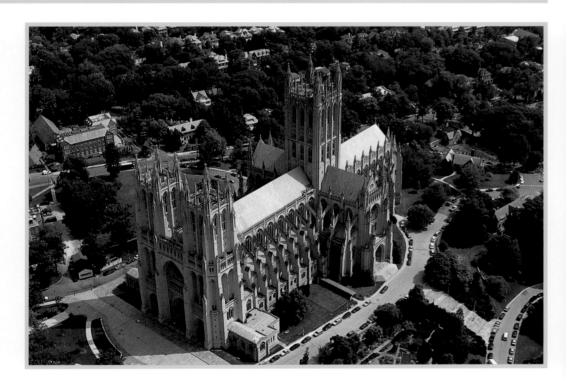

110-111 The handsome FedEx Stadium is the current home of the Washington Redskins, the capital's keenly followed football team.

111 The Kennedy Memorial Stadium can hold 56,500 people. In 1961, over 36,700 fans attended the first Washington Redskins game; it was against the New York Giants. It is nw a soccer stadium.

112 top and 112-113 A model of real-estate development common in Maryland in Virginia organizes homes in streets limited to residents only.

113 top In the Washington, D.C. area swimming pools and golf courses are close at hand everywhere. Many people consider the capital region to be a paradise for golfers, given its wide selection of clubs.

114-115 Since they offer more space and greenery, suburbs perfectly fit the American dream of the single-family home.

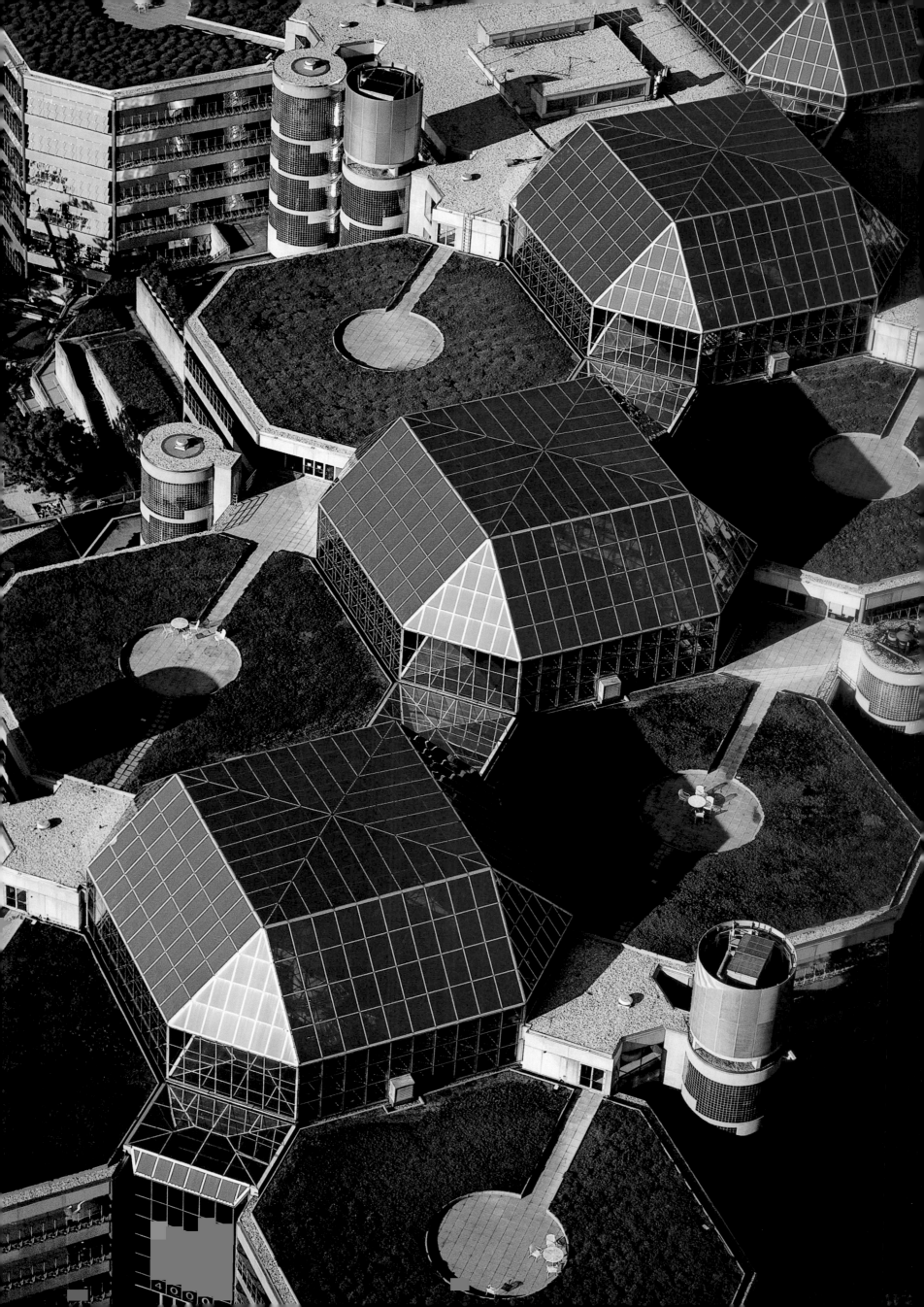

116 In 1985, the futuristic Intelsat Building on Connecticut Avenue became the headquarters of the company that launched the first commercial satellite.

117 The hanging gardens and the space-age domes of the Intelsat Building are among the complex's attractions; the structure houses offices, a health center, and a theater.

118-119 Jacob Funk bought land in 1765 which took his name, Funkstown. It is now Foggy Bottom where the circular Watergate complex and the Kennedy Center are located.

120-121 High-speed highways leading to the center and span the Washington Channel, created to keep the sea and overflow of the Fotomac under control.

122-123 The Key Bridge, which connects Georgetown to Virginia, is dedicated to Francis Scott Key, the author of the United States' national anthem. The flag that inspired it still exists.

124-125 Washington Harbor on the Washington Channel is a calm mooring place for the pleasure craft that crowd the Potomac on the weekends.

126-127 *The grassy area between the Washington Channel and the Potomac is the result of dredging done to clean that river that had degenerated into swampland. The area now forms Potomac Park.*

128-129 *The light streaming from automobile headlights and the shining marble and its reflections in the Potomac contribute to the magic of the night.*

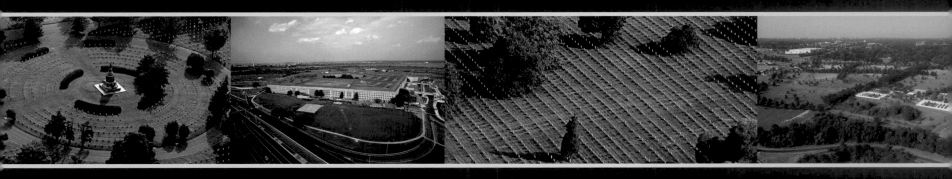

ARLINGTON

In Virginia, on the far side of the Potomac River, the District of Columbia's restrictions on the height of buildings, cease to be valid. Thus free, the County of Arlington shows no restraint in erecting apartment and office blocks, structures in cement and glass, buildings that are neither ugly nor impressive.

The only appeal of the suburbs is their low rents, their proximity to the city airport — Ronald Reagan National Airport — and their commercial abundance that satisfies the consumer whims of the capital. After nightfall they are just dormitory towns, except on the Fourth of July, when Washington experiences its only burst of nightlife. For Independence Day celebrations, in fact, the panoramic roofs of Rosslyn, the first town after Key Bridge, become a grandstand crowded with specta-

tors seeking a privileged view of the fireworks display on the Mall.

Arlington, however, is not merely a utilitarian outlet for the monumental splendor of Washington. It is, rather, a triumph of patriotism with its icons representing U.S. military force and the bravery of its soldiers. The town boasts the Pentagon and the most famous national cemetery of America.

The massive headquarters structure of the Department of Defense is most impressive from a bird's-eye view. Only from above it is possible to make out the five-sided geometrical shape, the Chinese box of five pentagons, one inside another other, the concentric repetition of barracks designed as walls of defense. The building also has five floors, as if the number had been ordained by some mysterious cabala. The propaganda handouts recite the key facts and figures with pride: the Pentagon is

132 top and 133 top
The Pentagon, one of the world's most instantly recognized buildings, is almost a city within itself (complete with helipad), offering a environment and an economy within itself.

132 bottom
A plane that has just taken off flies over the apparent calm of the Potomac River.

132-133 The bridge that physically re-united Washington

and Virginia (which were driven apart by the Civil War) was built between 1926 and 1932, in a Neoclassical design in keeping with the period's city planning.

GEORGETOWN

Built on the banks of the Potomac River, the historic town of Georgetown is a small city within the larger city. This small jewel jealously retains its Old European charm, with fine Georgian houses built by the wealthy merchants of the 1800s, the two-floor, 'federal' or Victorian-style townhouses of the middle class, and the narrow streets that climb up from the river as far as the gardens of Dumbarton Oaks.

Even before Pierre L'Enfant had conceived the capital, Georgetown was already an industrious commercial port and one of the main entrepôts for tobacco and grains grown on the region's rich plantations. The town's humble origins are barely perceptible in the district that attracts the capital's well-to-do elite — politicians and intellectuals, passing diplomats, young professionals, etc. Bordered on the south by the Potomac River, the area stretches out on the westernmost part of the district beyond Rock Creek, which flows unchecked through the wooded park of the same name that nestles within the town. "This place is undoubtedly the most pleasant of the whole county and the most suitable for settlement, wrote in 1634 Captain Henry Fleete, who traveled throughout the area trading furs and hides with the Indians. Here once stood Tahoga, a village of the Nacotchankes tribe, which, according to Thomas Jefferson, was also a meeting place of some forty tribes living between the Atlantic Ocean and the Potomac River.

After the Indians, the European colonies were also drawn to the area by the waterways surrounding it. Scottish merchants developed the flourishing tobacco trade. Barrels packed with the much-prized leaves were loaded onto British ships anchored in the port; tobacco was, in fact, used as money and even financed the construction of the town's first Presbyterian church. In the mid-18th century, in 1751, the 'Town of George' was officially baptized as a city. Its name, in actual fact, was not taken from the future president, George Washington, who was at the time an unknown youth in his twenties, but more likely from King George III of Great Britain. However, some versions suggest that the name may have been given to flatter two landowners in the area, George Gordon and George Beall, in the hope that they would donate some of their land. Absorbed in 1791 into the new federal city, the port provided easy access to the sites where the new capital's first buildings were erected. It continued to flourish until the mid-19th century, when railroad development and subsequently the eruption of the Civil War, marked the beginning of a gradual decline. The 1930s led to the aesthetic and cultural rediscov-

GEORGETOWN

144 *The Riggs Bank's gilded dome marks the crossing of M Street and Wisconsin Avenue, two busy Georgetown thoroughfares full of lively shops and elegant restaurants brimming with people.*

144-145 *Georgetown's tone is set by pleasant residential neighborhoods. Though some houses date back to the pre-Revolutionary era, most were built after 1870.*

145 top *On this section of Wisconsin Avenue, William Corcoran had a general store from which he started on his career as a philanthropist and art collector. He founded the downtown Corcoran Gallery of Art in 1859.*

145

146-147 *A house-top garden peaks out between the roofs of Victorian row houses. The historic homes in the neighborhood illustrate over a century of changing architectural tastes.*

ery of Old Georgetown. Nondescript and ramshackle huts were pulled down, the wooden and red brick houses were renovated and the fine homes were restored to their original splendor. The waterfront's historical heritage was preserved, as well as the adjoining area of mills, warehouses and factories. With the population increase in Washington the area took on greater importance, the prices of the houses began to rise, and Georgetown came back into fash-

146 bottom The modern architecture of Washington's new Potomac-waterfront has maintained the meticulous style and detailing of Georgetown's historical buildings.

147 Many of the shops along M Street have remained practically as they were in the early 19th century, with the shop on the ground floor and the office and homes on the upper floors. Today, however, most shopkeepers no longer live above their businesses.

148-149 Georgetown was a stylish neighborhood in the first half of the 19th century. It later declined with the bankruptcy of Chesapeake & Ohio Canal, and after World War I became one of the worst areas of the city. The popular stadium brings additional people and revenue to Georgetown.

150-151 The Key Bridge's reinforced cement structure is strengthened by spandrel arches. Unfortunately, its elevated feeder-highway, the Whitehurst Freeway, effectively destroyed the waterside for retail or recreational uses.

ion. Before becoming President of the United States John Fitzgerald Kennedy lived at No. 3307 N Street. In the neighborhood, in fact, it was not uncommon to encounter well-known political figures. Some claim to have seen Caspar Weinberger, when he was Secretary of Defense, pushing his shopping cart in the town's large Safeway supermarket, nicknamed 'Social Safeway' because its customers included such important figures (as well as those eager to meet them). In the same supermarket, in fact, King Abdullah of Jordan and his beautiful queen Rania are said to have been seen, in one of their few free moments during an official visit.

Anyone coming to Washington is eager to visit Georgetown. Europeans, especially, seem to fall in love with it, finding there the same pleasure of strolling through the streets in the evening that they enjoy in the historical centers of the Old Continent.

For well-to-do youth and the fashionable middle classes and for Washingtonians and visitors, Georgetown life is concentrated around the junction of M Street and Wisconsin Avenue, a neighborhood crowded with bars, ethnic restaurants, small antique shops, boutiques and period buildings transformed into elegant shopping centers. Right here, in the area where the latest trends are born and flourish, visitors can take a trip into the past through the gate of the Old Stone House, Washington's oldest standing house, built in 1765 in rough stone and brick, the only remaining example of 18th-century building.

Behind the hum of M Street is a quiet, residential area with an almost provincial, rural atmosphere enhanced by the little bridge and old steps leading down to the disused (but now restored) Chesapeake and Ohio Canal. Thus was designed in the second half of the 19th century to boost Washington's economic development. The

aim of the project, launched to the music of brass bands during the Fourth of July celebrations in 1829, was to join Chesapeake Bay in the north with the Ohio River and open the outlets of the Midwest. However, the project was never completed, being abandoned when railroads became the most econom-ic means of transport and new in-ternal waterways were no longer necessary. Today the canal, of which several locks still survive, is a picturesque attraction with pleas-ure boats that take visitors up and down its calm reaches, alongside the cyclists and joggers who follow the winding paths along its banks.

In Georgetown, the waters of Washington Harbor provide anoth-er oasis of relaxation. A stretch of terraces extends along the bank of the Potomac, with coffee bars and chic stores that are brightened up at night with multicolored fountains. Georgetown's fame, however, also includes a rather 'darker' attraction

152-153 Washington Harbor on the Potomac is a typical contemporary multi-use complex, offering offices, apartments, shops and restaurants in an attractive environment that emphasizes water, trees, and also big-city amenities.

153 top Luxury ferry boats now ply the waters of the Potomac: it was a very different type of ferry that John Wilkes Booth, Lincoln's assassin, used in 1865 in his attempted escape from Washington.

153 bottom On the Tidal Basin, a kiosk rents pedal boats which visitors can pedal up to the Jefferson Memorial. The artificial lake was used as a swimming pool until the middle of the 20th century.

154-155 Built in the 1980s, Washington Harbor successfully anticipated the shopping-winig-dining good-life syndrome that still attracts many visitors, both local and from afar.

– the 'Steps of Death' which feature in the film *The Exorcist*. This steep, narrow flight of steps cuts through between the walls of the houses built on the slope at the side of the canal; down them the exorcist priest (played by Max von Sidow) dramatically throws himself when the devil possesses him.

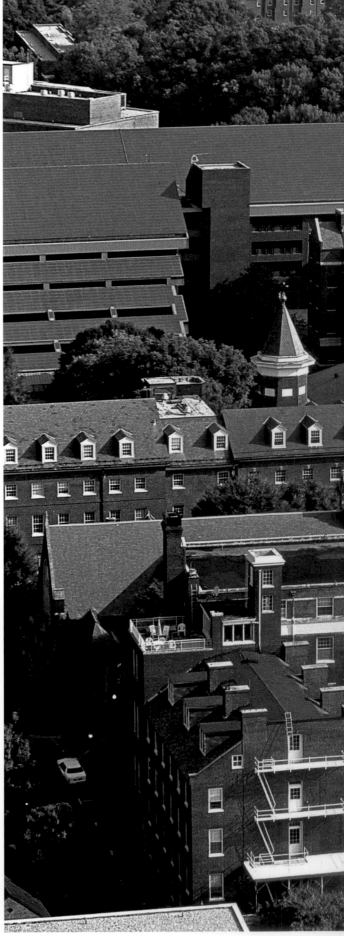

156 top
Georgetown
University enrolls
12,000 students
from 100 different
countries. Students
are required to live
on campus until
they are 21 years
old unless they live
with their families
in the city or
suburbs.

156 bottom
At Georgetown
University, athletic
activities are an
important part of
student life.
Competition is lively
in college events and
intense in events
against other
colleges.

156-157 Founded
in 1789,
Georgetown
University is the
oldest Catholic
university in the
United States. It has
been run by Jesuits
since 1805. The first
buildings were
constructed around
"the Old Quad."

158-159
Somewhere close to
the intersection of M
Street and
Wisconsin Avenue
stood Suter's Tavern,
where George
Washington signed
the enabling
document for the
federal capital. The
inn's exact location
is not known.